Seeing Voices:
Poetry in Motion

Seeing Voices:
Poetry in Motion

by

Kelly Sargent

Cover design by Shay Culligan

ISBN: 978-1-63980-135-0

Kelsay Books
502 South 1040 East, A-119
American Fork, Utah 84003
Kelsaybooks.com

For Renée Nicole,
my twin, my inspiration
(who still drinks Hawaiian Punch with me).

And to Leah and Kyle,
my children, my light
(who both preferred Berry Capri Sun).

Acknowledgments

Grateful acknowledgment is given to the following publications in which some of the included poems first appeared:

Cerasus Magazine: "Her Voice," "Fruits of Labor"

Poetic Sun: "Seeing Voices"

Stone Poetry Journal: "The Mushroom Caves in Madrid," "My Voice"

Vita Brevis Press: "Revelation"

Wingless Dreamer: "Night Vision"

Contents

Seeing Voices

My twin sister used to shut her eyes
to shut me up when we argued.
Born deaf, she held the advantage in any girlhood fight.
I had no choice but to be instantly
        muted;
her eyelids,
        a remote control when static sounded like me.

I would steady my hands in a signed
first-word-of-a-sentence,
poised to whip the air in a justified retort.
Hands tired in one position though:
    a pouting pinkie dangling from my palm.

If I caught her squinting one eye, I signed swiftly to get a word in,
    until
nut-brown eyelashes cemented once more,
silencing my voice,
sheathing my words without permission.

Tap, tap, tap on the shoulder:
    Listen to me.
Tap, tap, tap:
    I have something to say…

I'm sorry. I was wrong.
You'll never know if you don't open your eyes
    and hear me.

I'd reach out
to touch her hand.
I can't shout if I'm holding yours.
    Truce?

I miss her most on cloudy days.
I recall those rainy afternoons when we finger painted
under the kitchen's fluorescent bulb
and sipped Hawaiian Punch from smeared, aluminum cans;
quieter moments by necessity, but colored still
with goofy grins and funny red mustaches.

Sometimes
I slip away to my mirror in the bedroom
to see her nut-brown eyes gazing back at me.
I press my palm against the cool glass,
   just to touch her hand again.

Her Voice

I was born an identical twin in Luxembourg.
My miniature mirror followed me after I stretched our pungent means out
into a land perched on cliffs.
It's another girl, the makeshift midwife from next door must have announced
in French to a perspiring woman I would never call
  Mom.

My three-pound twin arrived unexpectedly
with a cry that she would never hear
  —she was deaf.

It wouldn't matter, though, that French words declared her
  a second
and an adoption agency asked nine months later if an American couple wanted to
trade her in.
One day,
  she would hear
with the nut-brown eyes, then lidded shut,
and speak a language that was already foreign to them;

foreign because they had four ears that weren't broken,
  or because

they had four ears
that were   broken.

I have one broken and one not,

but I didn't know which one was which
until 23 minutes ago
      when I considered it.

The ten tiny fingers she must have clenched
that would one day be
     her voice
differed eloquently from the vibrations in her throat
that assuredly joined in chorus with mine
to fill that stuffy, damp and narrow room.

I wonder if the sweaty stranger or her neighbor counted them.

The Mushroom Caves in Madrid

remember when we descended the dank hollow,
hollow like the cool, clay ashtrays cradling
the spent brown butts
we found cowering behind the whiskey bottle

that they swilled in the mushroom caves
following the bullfight

and you huddled at the foot of my bed in the tangy orange afghan
we shared
after the beast trickled blood uncauterized that night

in the pen dusted crimson.

you liked the banderilla's pink crêpe paper;
we willed it pretty.

we crawled under the table, sticky
oak legs spread wide,
swollen, soaked, and stiff.
garlic burned more than sangria.

my twin, my deaf mirror,
sign with your tiny hands and

tell me:
what time are we allowed to eat stuffed mushrooms?

Devouring Grace

The Little Bear,
grand and grey and nestled in the fountain basin,
waved his immobile paw to my twin and me

as we neared the Chinese restaurant
every single time
in the middle of smoky, sweaty, star-lit Madrid.

Named by foreign, five-year-old twins,
unbuckled
in the back of a banged-up, midnight-blue German VW,

he was doomed to endure a perpetual bath;
        his in surely putrid, cloudy bath water,

and my twin and I shivered sympathetic strands of sorrow
        over his pitiful plight.

And then, we arrived at The River of Pearl,
    famished,
needing to sate our
        hunger.

He knew that we would.

I didn't think to think it odd to crave
Chinese spare ribs and greasy rice,
        fried in the middle of Madrid,
until long after we had moved away
        to yet another
    foreign land.

And then, I did.

Memories aren't memories until they are recalled;
nor are five-year-old twins lost
until they are found.

I wonder if the Little Bear still waves to little girls,
unbuckled,
under the stars.

Fruits of Labor

I wrap your tiny hand around my throat,
size identical to your own,
for you to feel the sounds vibrating within:

blue-ber-ry

ba-nan-a

straw-ber-ry

You wrap your tiny hand around your throat,
size identical to my own,
for you to mimic the vibrations
that form the consonants and the vowels that you cannot hear.

Your index finger with the Snoopy Band-Aid
            searches for the *"r-r-r"*...

blue-ber-ry?

I shake my head. *Look at my lips,* I sign.

blue-ber-ry

I watch the cherry Chapstick crack on your lips
    as "blueberry" makes them pucker.

Next,
ba-nan-a?

Umm, say it slower, I say. *See my tongue?*

You mimic and mash *"n-n-n"* against the roof of your mouth
   with a tentative nod and raised, hopeful eyebrows.

Then,
straw-ber-ry?

Hand on my hip.
     Hmm, remember Dr. Lane
         with her popsicle stick? Ahhh ...

But you open too wide.

We cover our mouths momentarily to stifle girlish giggles —
   We are, after all, hard at work.

blue-ber-ry

ba-nan-a

straw-ber-ry

         and repeat:
blue-ber-ry

ba-nan-a

straw-ber-ry

         and adjust:
blue-ber-ry

ba-nan-a

straw-ber-ry

                           and tweak:

blue-ber-ry

ba-nan-a

straw-ber-ry

                         again
                         and again
                         and again

   and once more

until—

        fruit never tasted
          so sweet
        in our mouths.

Night Vision

On the other side of midnight lies a twin in my mirror.
I glimpse her raven eyes,
taunting me: *I-SAW, I-SAW*...

Illuminated by truth colored indigo—
that ancient, integritous color that managed to slip
    between two cones
and settle devotedly,
    unnamed for so long—

she crosses

intuitively between night and day
with starved, skinny, bird-like arms,
    erect and at attention.
Hands with pointy fingernails claw at my skin.

A ghostly, peppermint-peppered breath
sucked cool in my throat
    whispers silver strands of grace,

and shadowed truths
 slip
into blinding night vision.

Her pupils dilate remorse,
 and we blink away Night.

We sip the moon's warm milk
that reminds us of childhood tales in the dark before slumber.
We toast to midnight.

And then,
we see dewdrops on wakened leaves…
Morning mourns the midnight moon.

Rumors of Spring

An empty checkered vase rests on the shelf,
   dusty,
and long abandoned.

You once were a bud,
   and I held you.

Though divine in design
   and regal in intention,

you sipped water
   from modest, tiny roots;

an unkept promise.

Even near sunlight
you lived in a shadow,
   dependent upon movements of
hands
   on a clock.

Until,
   a nascent meadow revealed itself
   beyond our paned window,

cradling twins of another kind.

You tentatively took leave,

and found your place.

Sunlight illuminated you
   and struck you
      luminescent.

I watched you play in teal-tinted rains
and marveled as your auburn hair
absorbed autumn's last dusk.

You were named
as nature had promised.

And soon,
with rumors of spring made real,

You

bloomed.

Kissing the Horizon

Barefoot
on the beach swings,
we used to watch the horizon bob—
  where sunset unfolds in sleepy, dusty-rose hues
and sunrise yawns,
  stretching golden limbs to greet the day.

The sun kissed the horizon that night,
preparing to bid us graceful farewell
  with a promise to awaken us gently in a morning embrace.

Twilight rapped,
and we answered.
We engaged Night.

Moon's obsession with the seas made solemn its ascension.
Eager winds wrestled for domination.
Distant mountains turned submissive
and acquiesced their muscular contours.

Cradled in wispy silver threads
cast by a spool of smattered stars, we were
wrapped securely in a vast, uninterrupted galaxy.

But holding the rusty chains on the swings
with both hands
made us mute.

Starlight wasn't enough.

Lip-reading,
  too fragile a tether.

Tonight, swaddled by near-darkness,
I nestle on a chilled, tide-weathered beach
that swallows my memories
    carelessly.
Sand slips between my fingers
like unspoken words on my hands.

At first light,
revelation kisses the horizon.

A mourning dove coos,
   pausing
      to remember.

Revelation

Beside my cabin, a reflection shimmers
on humid luminescence
that bewitches me curiously within,
captivating me against my will.

The brazen luster measures without apology
my depths and my shallows
without my consent,
revealing secrets I've kept surreptitiously hidden
from sunlight

that continues to remain loyal
whether I deserve it or not.

Entranced in a mesmeric gaze, we eye one another
uneasily
until a dragonfly skims the surface
and breaks the enchantment.
I am revealed in ripples that disseminate
an imperfect nature.

The Quaking Aspen

A Quaking Aspen tree roots devotedly
in the resplendent woods behind my childhood home,
a curious anomaly among the Royal Red Maples
blazing stunning crimson, sultry summer days all.
Striking round leaves tremble
even in the gentlest, well-intentioned breeze,
shuddering like wings on hastened monarchs at dusk.
Butterflies with cleverly-inked wings
chance upon a kindred mirror
in my childhood woods many a day.

Then, in apple-sweetened, autumn air
this singular, staggering, spectacular beauty unlike another
bequeaths us gold.

Beauty "out of this world," Mother used to say.
"Only God can make something dying so breathtaking."

There once had stood two.

Dawn curtsies, and I weave the woods, recalling the ghost of my
twin sister
by my side, gauzy fingers fluttering in a brittle breeze.

I shuffle at stubborn crabgrass long covering trails
once carved by four leather sandal soles.
She always wore red.
Parents too easily hoodwinked by identical, ten-year-old imps
had colored me blue.

I had dutifully counted aloud, every time, though she never heard
my voice.
Born deaf, her eyes were her ears.

My beloved had blended easily in her hiding places,
hugging trees
while I skipped the numbers from 3 to 7 before I sought her.

I seek her still.
My mirror.
I seek it, still.

"Your turn to count," I signed. "No peeking."
Her ears closed.
I heard a crack that she did not.

I saw a crimson canopy part reverently for the retreating golden
wonder among them.

Dappled sunlight through crestfallen leaves framed her properly-
princessed visage.

Nearly encased.
Fit for royalty.
A coffin gold.

And red, of course;
she always wore red.

Only God could make something dying so
devastatingly
breath-taking.

Fingers twitched momentarily—to utter a final word?

In my childish ignorance I imagined:
"Now I lay me down to sleep."

Abed, she was.

A mourning dove cried from afar…
                    It's you, *it cooed,* it's you.
Mourning doves, they mate for life.

Mother spotted her twins at dusk,
  asleep too far back in the woods.
  Cold.
"I called for nearly an hour," she choked.

I'm deaf, I discovered.
My mirror is me, and I am my mirror.
Now I lay me down to sleep.

Fingers that had spoken final words trace a branch
  split, still hovering just above the ground.
    ...No peeking.

Damp sorrow clings to leaves that tremble,
sympathetic as they always were.
The mourning dewdrops refract eerie light into silky strands of
grace.
I glimpse a ghostly reflection.

Caught in a web woven inside the hollow of a
  long-forgotten,
  long-remembered Aspen log,
frail, sticky memories trapped
…peek.

Remember me.

The web flutters in a brisk, blessed breeze.
Reflections find no home
  amid the absence of dust,
     once settled to shelter scattered memories.

Mirror shards stream blood
  traversing desperately in search of cracked, split lips
parched for baptismal water.

...Now I lay her down to sleep.

I watch a butterfly skim a dewdrop.
The fallen branch offers her respite.
  She alights.
Her wings flutter red.

My fingers
      brush gauziness away,
               ...and I wave back.

My Voice

I am Deaf.
My fingers speak.

A coiffed paintbrush in my grasp,
my voice streaks turquoise and magenta
  across a parched canvas.
Vowels coo through thirsty linen.

Click-clacking keys with my mother tongue,
  I chew hard consonants
and spit them out.
Sour, a scathing sonnet can be at dusk.

Fingertips pave slick exclamations,
punctuated by nails sinking low into clamminess.
I sculpt hyperboles.

Poetry in Motion

Though the light is dim,
deafness need not flavor our reunion.
Twilight colors our handheld voices.

Swallowing candlelight that graces the table,
the glowing appetizer warms our throats
as we feast wide eyes on sweet and savory dishes
    meant to linger in our bellies until long after midnight.

Sipping from crystals imbibed
with rosé for me and white for you,
we grow giddy between samples of moonlight,
  creamy and smooth on crisp linen.

Fingers spin tales before firelight
    as silver-bangled spools unwind syllables
        and pastel-polished nails paint on invisible canvases.
Finger foods must remain a while longer on napkins...

There are stories to tell.

About the Author

Born hard of hearing and adopted in Luxembourg, Kelly Sargent grew up with a deaf twin sister in Europe and the United States. She has written for *SIGNews,* a national newspaper for the Deaf, and worked in educational settings with deaf students. Her poetry and artwork in the past year, including a Best of the Net nominee, appeared in more than thirty literary publications in the U.S. and abroad. She serves as the creative nonfiction editor and an assistant nonfiction editor for two literary journals, as well as an editor for an international poetry anthology publisher. She also reviews for a literary magazine dedicated to making visible the artistic expression of sexual violence survivors. Residing in picturesque Vermont with her family, she also enjoys writing stories for children. A children's book entitled *Sundae Sundays* is due out later this year.